Exploring Growing with God

Personal and group material
exploring Spiritual Growth
in Individuals and Churches

by

Colin Smith

MOORLEY'S Print & Publishing

© Copyright 2005

All rights reserved. No part of this publication may be reproduced, stored in a retrieval system, or transmitted, in any form or by any means, electronic, mechanical, photocopying, recording or otherwise, without the prior written permission of the Publisher.

British Library Cataloguing in Publication Data.
A catalogue record for this book is available from the British Library.

ISBN 0 86071 581 7

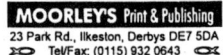

MOORLEY'S Print & Publishing
23 Park Rd., Ilkeston, Derbys DE7 5DA
Tel/Fax: (0115) 932 0643

All Scripture quotations are taken from the *Holy Bible, New International Version,* Copyright © 1973, 1978, 1984 by International Bible Society. Used by permission of Hodder & Stoughton Ltd

Contents

Foreword		5
Introduction		7
Session One:	The Philippian Jailer	11
Session Two:	Personal Growth	19
Session Three:	The Growing Church	27
Session Four:	Growing the Church	37
Session Five:	The Sower	47
Session Six:	Further Bible Passages	53

Foreword

"Exploring growing with God" began life as a set of photocopied notes for a church weekend away. No-one was more surprised than me to be asked to lead four lengthy sessions for Town End Methodist Church, Chapel-en-le Frith, for I hardly felt qualified to do so. True I am a Local Preacher of some 15 years experience, and my "tent making" takes place in a University context, but this was quite different. I would be exposing my ideas, my spirituality and indeed my whole self to a group of lively, mature and questioning Christians.

I was pleasantly surprised both by the blessings received in its preparation, and by how well it was appreciated by the group. Although I make no claims to originality, new insights have been gained into the growth of *both individuals and churches*, and profitably shared amongst us. In a sense therefore the book has been tried and tested, and so I feel confident in offering it to a wider audience. I pray that re-presenting the material in book form will stimulate thought, action and growth in its readers and their church.

I would like to offer my thanks to:

>The Rev. David E Youngs, Superintendent minister (at the time) of the then Whaley Bridge Circuit,
>
>Colin Briant, who led me to Christ all those years ago, and to
>
>My wife Irene, who has put up with my neglect of house and home to undertake tasks such as this.

Therefore, dear friends, ...grow in the grace and knowledge of our Lord and Saviour Jesus Christ. To him be glory both now and forever! Amen.
2 Peter 3: 17-18.

Colin Smith

Introduction

The process of growth

Physical growth is a natural and familiar process, which is often used in the Bible as a metaphor for spiritual growth. Both Jesus and the apostle Paul, for instance, use the familiarity of physical growth to teach us about spiritual growth. One of Jesus's most powerful parables was that of the sower, where he unusually went to great lengths to give a careful explanation of its meaning (see Matt 13:1-23). And the purpose of many of Paul's letters was to encourage the growth of both individuals and churches (see, for example, 1 Cor 3:1-3).

There are strong similarities between the two processes. Both arise from small beginnings and need ongoing careful nurture. Perhaps less obvious to us in this scientific age – they also require the active participation of both humankind and of God himself. As we explore growth, we will discover more and more evidence of His creative activity in the lives of human beings. Furthermore, we will become more and more aware that we are privileged for he allows us to participate with him in this creative activity.

Perspective on growth

The chapters which follow make no pretence at being innovative. Our explorations, however, are made from a particular perspective and with some presuppositions. The main concern, for example, is not primarily with methodology. Methodology is of course important. We need to know what others have done and found successful, so that we can evaluate their methods for our own use both in our individual quest for growth, and for the growth of the church to which we belong. But the conviction here is that prior to choosing what to do we would benefit from exploring the process itself, as it works itself out in both our individual and corporate lives. We therefore focus more upon what is actually going on inside both individuals and churches as they grow spiritually.

So let us be patient. We have a perfectly natural and good inclination to "get on with it", since we are anxious for both our own and our church's growth to be both rapid and visible. It is my conviction however that it is worth investing a little time in exploring the process, so that our actions can be more surely undertaken in partnership with God.

Presuppositions

Our first presupposition is that there are two dimensions to growth, which interact with each other. The first is growth in our relationship with God as we get to know Him better. This shows itself in daily living, where the fruits of the Spirit (Gal 5:22) become more and more manifest. As we become more like Him, so our concern for others becomes stronger and we are more able to play our part in meeting their needs. This growth in relationships with others is the second dimension of growth. It works the other way around too – as we step forth in faith, to help others, we find that He is there before us. We meet Him in each situation of need (Matt 25:40), and our relationship with him is thereby strengthened. The second dimension of growth flows from the first dimension, and the first dimension itself is fed by the second.

These two dimensions of growth are sometimes pictured as a growth upward, and a growth outward to form a cross (Figure 1).

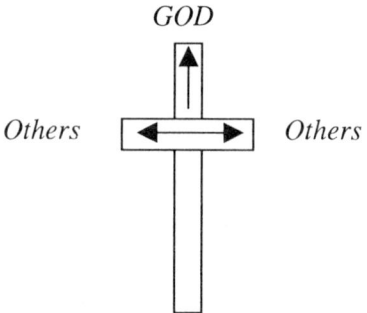

Figure 1 – The two dimensions of growth

The second presupposition is that there is an interaction between the growth of individuals and of the church to which they belong. A church needs to provide situations whereby its members *can* grow. This means things like home groups, bible fellowships, weekday prayers and opportunities to co-operate with Christ in his work within the community. As individuals within the church take these opportunities, so the Holy Spirit is more able to use them. They thereby have a greater impact on those around them, and the church grows. Individual Christians can best grow within such a church, and a church needs growing Christians in its ranks if it is itself to grow. These interactions can be represented cyclically (Figure 2).

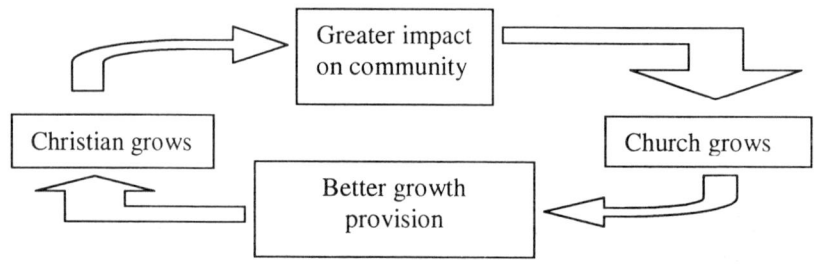

Figure 2 – Cyclical interactions

Finally there are presuppositions about our God. He loves to teach us and wants us to grow – but He respects our free will and will not push us into anything until we are ready. And when we are ready, we can rely upon Him to be alongside us, offering as much help as we need. All we have to do is accept it. At no point in the process of growth does anyone need to feel under pressure. Our explorations should therefore be approached prayerfully with a spirit of openness to his guidance, knowing he is alongside us.

Overview of this book

Both the perspective and presuppositions above are explored in the following chapters.

- *Session 1* - The Philippian Jailer is a case study based upon Acts16: 16-34. This case study is particularly apt because the time taken to grow into faith from initial enquiry to full acceptance is relatively short, and it illustrates some important points to be considered in later chapters.

- *Session 2* – Personal growth - uses part of the first chapter of Paul's letter to the Colossians (Col 1:9-13) to study what happens next i.e. after the new birth. It is basically about Paul's desire that Christians should grow – particularly in wisdom and understanding.

- *Session 3* – Church growth - shows a change of focus. The main concern here (Acts 2:41-7) is to identify the characteristics of a growing church rather than a growing individual, whilst remembering that the two are related (Figure 2 above).

- *Session 4* – Growing the church - is about witness, both the witness of the individual and of the church corporately. It is based upon Acts 1:6-8. It also suggests a model of the process of mission as a precursor to choosing appropriate methodologies for a particular church.

- *Session 5* – The Sower – rounds off these reflections through a detailed look at the parable of the sower (Matt 13:1-9 and 18-23). This is an encouraging parable about receptiveness and different states of mind.

- *Session 6* – Further reading – a few further passages of scripture are suggested here.

Ways to use this book.

This book can simply be used as a good devotional read for a committed Christian. However, in all forms of Bible study it is important to give adequate time to stop and think about what has been read. Therefore at the end of each chapter there are suggestions for individual reflection. I hope you find them useful.

It may also be used in a number of ways for group Bible study. Therefore, there are questions, also at the end of each chapter, which are intended to gently provoke thought and prayer in a group context. Use and adapt them, as feels right. Naturally, much depends on the style and aims of the individual group.

Session One

The Philippian Jailer

God acts in people's lives - sometimes in a spectacular way – to bring them to the point of making a decision about their future. Paul's Jailer in Acts 16:16-34 is one such case.

Like physical growth, spiritual growth requires both a conception and a birth. The spiritual birth is generally taken as the point at which a full commitment is made – or at which a person realises that they are fully committed. In physical birth there is a growth in the womb, which usually takes some nine months or so. A similar growth occurs prior to spiritual birth but the time scale varies tremendously from person to person. In the case of the jailer the time scale appears to be very short indeed. Nonetheless growth occurs, and the features of that growth are well worth noting.

Let us now read through the story, and then ponder, little by little what is happening and what its significance is.

Acts 16:16-34

[16] *Once when we were going to the place of prayer, we were met by a slave girl who had a spirit by which she predicted the future. She earned a great deal of money for her owners by fortune telling.* [17] *This girl followed Paul and the rest of us, shouting, "These men are servants of the Most High God, who are telling you the way to be saved."* [18] *She kept this up for many days. Finally Paul became so troubled that he turned round and said to the spirit, "In the name of Jesus Christ I command you to come out of her!" At that moment the spirit left her.*

[19] *When the owners of the slave girl realised that their hope of making money was gone, they seized Paul and Silas and dragged them into the market-place to face the authorities.* [20] *They brought them before the magistrates and said, "These men are Jews, and are throwing our city into an uproar* [21] *by advocating customs unlawful for us Romans to accept or practice."*

[22] *The crowd joined in the attack against Paul and Silas, and the magistrates ordered them to be stripped and beaten.* [23] *After they had been severely flogged, they were thrown into prison, and the jailer was commanded to guard them carefully.* [24] *Upon receiving such orders, he put them in the inner cell and fastened their feet in the stocks.*

[25] *About midnight Paul and Silas were praying and singing hymns to God,*

and the other prisoners were listening to them. ²⁶ *Suddenly there was such a violent earthquake that the foundations of the prison were shaken. At once all the prison doors flew open, and everybody's chains came loose.* ²⁷ *The jailer woke up, and when he saw the prison doors open, he drew his sword and was about to kill himself because he thought the prisoners had escaped.* ²⁸ *But Paul shouted, "Don't harm yourself! We are all here!"*

²⁹ *The jailer called for lights, rushed in and fell trembling before Paul and Silas.*

³⁰ *He then brought them out and asked, "Sirs, what must I do to be saved?"*

³¹ *They replied, "Believe in the Lord Jesus, and you will be saved — you and your household."*

³² *Then they spoke the word of the Lord to him and to all the others in his house.* ³³ *At that hour of the night the jailer took them and washed their wounds; then immediately he and all his family were baptised.* ³⁴ *The jailer brought them into his house and set a meal before them, and the whole family was filled with joy, because they had come to believe in God.*

The context of the story is the casting out of a spirit from a fortune telling slave girl. We need not concern ourselves here with the nature of the spirit, but the spectacular healing provoked a response not only from her owners, but also from the crowd and the local magistrates.

The owners reacted as they did because they would now lose the large income which they had previously received from the girl. The magistrates could see the beginnings of uproar so they acted immediately to quell it. It is less clear why "the crowd" responded in the way they did. Some would certainly need to keep well in with the magistrates and the slave owners. Others may simply have feared the supernatural and responded hastily to rid themselves of Paul and Silas. If these strangers could do that – what else might they do?

But there would have been still others for whom this looked like a sign of the presence of God. Or who suddenly started to think that there might be a God after all. Some of these would have slipped off home to tell their families and friends. Perhaps the jailer was one who heard in this way?

We will of course never know for sure, we are simply not told. But it is worth noting that it is perhaps not such a sudden conversion as appears at first sight.

Let us now consider the rest of the story in more detail.

Verse 25

[25] *About midnight Paul and Silas were praying and singing hymns to God, and the other prisoners were listening to them.*

What a witness Paul and Silas gave from their prison cell at Philippi!

There they were with painful, bleeding bodies in a vermin-infested cell, praying and singing to the glory of God. The other prisoners, the account says, were listening to them. Listening with puzzlement, no doubt, for groans of pain and curses would have been more normal.

We are reminded of Terry Waite's experience of unjust imprisonment in the Lebanon. It wasn't easy but he came through it. In his case, one of the most helpful things he found was the liturgy of his church. There were so many prayers that he knew by heart that he was able to use them often – and they uplifted him. *We are promised the strength we need at the time we need it.* We see this both in Paul and Silas, and in Terry's experience. Dare we also say that growth took place through the singing of the hymns and the saying of the prayers in these cases?

Verse 26

Suddenly there was such a violent earthquake that the foundations of the prison were shaken. At once all the prison doors flew open, and everybody's chains came loose.

There was an earthquake – and there is nothing particularly unusual about that in Philippi. Apparently Philippi is built on a fault-line, so minor quakes could well have been common. But this quake was a particularly big one, and it frightened both the jailer and his prisoners.

It was so big that it shook open the doors of the jail and released the prisoners from their fetters. They were freed. It was a natural event, but at exactly the time needed to enable Paul and Silas to continue their ministry. It would not be an exaggeration to call it a miraculous coincidence – the hand of God is clearly at work here.

Verse 27a

[27] *The jailer woke up*

With all the singing and the shaking that was going on, it is not surprising that the jailer woke! To him, the case of Paul and Silas would have been routine. It was alleged that they were going around stirring up trouble by preaching a message that was anti-Roman and so they had ended up in his jail. There is nothing particularly surprising about that. We have similar rules today. We do not allow people to incite riots, and persistent troublemakers may well find themselves spending a night in our police cells, or longer in one of our prisons.

But, what sort of a job was it being a jailer? Ever since people began living together in communities, there have been people who break the rules of those communities and are kept separate for a while. Therefore, he would certainly have no fear of unemployment. In today's terms he had it made – regular pay for the rest of his life, reasonable housing, well respected in the community etc. This makes this story particularly apt. Some people today also feel secure in what they do, and consequently think they have no need of religion. They too could well be in for a shock.

But there was a particular problem in the case of the Philippian Jailer.

Verses 27b and 28
and when he saw the prison doors open, he drew his sword and was about to kill himself because he thought the prisoners had escaped.
²⁸ But Paul shouted, "Don't harm yourself! We are all here!"

The jailer was thrown into a blind panic. It is not difficult to see why. A jailer in an ancient prison was completely responsible for his prisoners. If they escaped, the jailer paid for his failure with his life. And it would not necessarily be a quick death. Realising the prison doors were open, the jailer assumed all the prisoners had escaped. Not only did he stand to lose his livelihood, his family, his home, but his life itself in a nasty and painful way.

Suicide was the better option for him. The earthquake had provoked a crisis in his life, which he did not know how to handle. It is still so today. There are still people who are unable to cope with crises, often of a much less intense nature, and who consider suicide rather than go on. Let us give thanks for the work of the "Samaritans" and others, who stand alongside people in these circumstances.

So the jailer was not so secure after all. After years of thinking that his life was all mapped out and that he could look forward to living happily ever after, suddenly it was all threatened and he discovered that he had nothing to fall back on. He was outwardly secure – but inwardly fragile. We may feel like that or there may be people around us, for whom events have shaken their view of their own future. God can use such situations to bring people to him – and to provoke a further phase of growth in those who know him already.

Verses 29 and 30
²⁹ The jailer called for lights, rushed in and fell trembling before Paul and Silas.
³⁰ He then brought them out and asked, "Sirs, what must I do to be saved?"

The jailer, thoroughly unnerved, rushes into the inner prison and kneels before his prisoners. From his lips comes an ageless cry: "What must I do to be saved?"

There seems to be at least <u>two</u> sorts of reasons for the jailer's appeal to Paul and Silas. First of all, the earthquake and the threat of a painful death pushed the jailer towards action. Millions of people similarly have turned toward God through helplessness in the face of experiences, which they cannot handle. So they cry out for deliverance. They are being pushed into His loving arms.

Figure 3 - *Pushes and pulls to faith*

Secondly the attitudes and actions of Paul and Silas pull him towards faith. Their calm demeanour and worshipful response must have impressed him, coming as it did after they had been stripped, flogged and taken a severe beating. Furthermore, when the earthquake came they stayed where they were so as not to endanger his life. This was a quality of life he had not seen before and instinctively he longed to be like them. There is a power in the normal Christian life, as it is lived out in the full view of others.

The jailer was both "<u>pushed</u>" and "<u>pulled</u>" toward faith in Jesus Christ. Is this your experience too?

Verses 31 and 32
³¹ They replied, "Believe in the Lord Jesus, and you will be saved — you and your household."
³² Then they spoke the word of the Lord to him and to all the others in his house.

Becoming a Christian means believing in the Lord Jesus Christ. It is important to grasp what this means. "Believing" in the New Testament sense means more than accepting an intellectual proposition. It involves the trust of a living relationship. It means that life becomes centred on and lived out in relationship with Jesus. Thus a personal commitment to Him is necessary. By commitment a door is opened and God is allowed in to begin His work of grace within us. We cannot save ourselves. All is of God. All He needs is for us to invite Him in and to allow him to do so.

In short believing in the Lord Jesus brings a new and enduring quality of life available to all. It is referred to in the New Testament as "eternal life".

Verse 33

[33] At that hour of the night the jailer took them and washed their wounds; then immediately he and all his family were baptised. [34] The jailer brought them into his house and set a meal before them, and the whole family was filled with joy, ...se they had come to believe in God.

... of the jailer on becoming a Christian was to ease pain, by binding up the wounds of Paul and Silas. A few hours earlier his only concern was fastening them up so they couldn't escape. Now he is washing their wounds, and sharing his food with them.

The jailer's actions should be no surprise to us. No one else has released such a flood of compassion into the stream of history as Jesus, mainly through the concern of individual Christians, expressing their love of God in love for their neighbours. The jailer's character had changed. Such is the power of the gospel in people's lives. His newly found Christianity immediately showed itself in a practical concern for the needs of others and a generosity beyond the call of duty.

Summary

That then is the story of the Philippian jailer. The three things which impacted most powerfully on my thinking, as I wrote this, are:
- the witness of Paul and Silas singing and praying whilst in jail,
- the earthquake provoking a crisis in the jailer's life, and
- the response of the jailer to the gospel call.

But what does it teach us about growth? A number of things come to my mind, the most important of which are:
- Growth is initiated by pushes and pulls within our life experiences.
- Growth occurs as we respond to those pushes and pulls by trusting more in God.
- Growth results in an increased concern for others and for God.
- Growth often arises from the impact of individual Christians on each other and on those around them.

Do you agree?

Personal reflection
Give thanks for the story of the Philippian jailer and for any particular points which struck you on reading it. However, it was all a long time ago. So it may be useful to think about a more modern example. Think of yourself as the modern case study.

Was your coming to faith sudden or was it slow and gradual?

What "drivers" were important? Can you identify both push (earthquake, crisis etc) and pull (attractive Christian people or actions) factors?

Does this tell you anything about our mission today?

What is your vision for the future for yourself?

Are you growing?

Work through the group questions below as far as you are able.

Group Questions
The questions below are offered as discussion starters. However, some ask for a personal response. Please be willing to share as much as you feel comfortable with, but equally do not feel under pressure to do so. Similarly feel free to omit questions that you do not find helpful.

1. What have you found i) encouraging, ii) discouraging about the story of the Philippian jailer?

2. You come across a person (younger than yourself) who is in distress over a family crisis. You try to help, and in the course of the conversation you talk about how your faith has helped you at times of crisis. A few days later you are visited by an angry parent (or spouse or close friend), who accuses you of taking advantage of the person's weakness, of using an emotional appeal at a time of greatest vulnerability.
    Defend yourself against this allegation.
    Wasn't this what Paul and Silas were doing with the jailer?

3. *"Believe in the Lord Jesus, and you will be saved."* What are we really saying when we call Jesus Lord?

4. Even the devil believes in Jesus. Is belief then really enough?

5. What does it mean to be saved? What does it mean to you in your life?

6. How much did the jailer understand about what he was getting into? How much did he need to know?

7. What can we learn from the story of the Philippian jailer, about our mission today?

8. There are other kinds of prisons. Some people for example are trapped by compulsive habits or live with chronic anxiety from which they cannot escape. Is this, or has this ever been true of you or someone you know? Share your experience. What can people in these situations learn from Paul and Silas?
9. Can we prepare for unexpected major crises in our own lives? How?
10. How can we apply what we have learnt about growth to our own lives?

Quietly pray together – *silently or aloud - as you feel moved. Rest quietly in him, aware of his presence. He will guide your prayers. He will prompt you when the time comes to close the session. It may be helpful if one person simply starts with the words "Let us pray", and closes the session after a suitable interval by announcing the grace. Before you start, think together about what you are going to pray about.*

Session Two

Personal Growth

The Philippian Jailer committed himself forever to a living relationship with God – but that would not be the end of the story. The next step would be for him to join a church within which he could grow. We know there was a church in Philippi at that time, because we are told of Lydia's house fellowship there in Acts 16:40. My guess therefore is that he and his family joined that house fellowship and grew in faith and love for the rest of their lives – though of course we will never know for sure.

In this chapter, we are going to think about the growth of Christians within a church. To do so we are going to think about a particular passage in Paul's letter to the Colossians – Col 1:9-14: This gives us clues about desirable features of growth.

But first, a little background is necessary. Paul spent a lot of time travelling, and on this occasion had Timothy with him as a friend and companion. So when he uses the plural "we" he is referring to himself and Timothy. Secondly, neither of them had any direct knowledge of the Colossian church since they had never travelled there. This meant it would be difficult for Paul and Timothy to be specific in their prayers or advice for the faithful brothers of Colosse. Their prayers are such as might be said for anyone – including us!

Colossians 1: 9-14

[9] For this reason, since the day we heard about you, we have not stopped praying for you and asking God to fill you with the knowledge of his will through all spiritual wisdom and understanding. [10] And we pray this in order that you may live a life worthy of the Lord and may please him in every way: bearing fruit in every good work, growing in the knowledge of God, [11] being strengthened with all power according to his glorious might so that you may have great endurance and patience, and joyfully [12] giving thanks to the Father, who has qualified you to share in the inheritance of the saints in the kingdom of light. [13] For he has rescued us from the dominion of darkness and brought us into the kingdom of the Son he loves, [14] in whom we have redemption, the forgiveness of sins.

Let us work our way through the passage, looking for advice on our personal growth.

Verse 9a
since the day we heard about you, <u>we have not stopped praying for you</u>

Paul takes heed of the parable of the persistent widow as given by Jesus in Luke 18:1-8, by being persistent in his prayer. If we are to grow in our relationship with God then we too need to pray regularly and persistently not allowing ourselves to become impatient or discouraged, but rather gently "keeping at it".

Like many things in the life of faith, this is easier said than done. But as we "keep at it" we find that our love for others grows, our intercessory prayer gains importance, and it is no hardship to pray persistently. We do however need to be realistic – we soon find that we cannot pray for every concern, every day. So, we must allow the Holy Spirit to guide us both as to who to pray for and how often. Personally, I have developed a weekly cycle of intercessory prayer, where each day focuses upon particular individuals or concerns. A daily list of urgent and particularly important matters supplements this. Perhaps Paul had something similar?

Verse 9b
asking God to fill you with the knowledge of his will...

Paul's main concern is that they might be filled with knowledge of the will of God. He therefore clearly links growth with knowing the will of God. This means that they will have to learn to listen to Him more and more. Indeed as we grow we become aware that prayer is not so much trying to make God listen to us, as trying to make ourselves listen to Him.

Part of our process of growth must therefore be learning to listen to God – but what does this mean? Few of us hear voices directly, so when we talk about listening to God we are, for the most part, talking metaphorically. The "voice of God", in fact, comes to us in many different ways. It has been said that the second thought is the word of God. In other words, assume you are quiet before God and you are seeking His will about something. The first thought that pops into your mind will be "of yourself", and the second one will be God speaking to you.

Personally I don't altogether believe that! But it does suggest that one way we listen to the voice of God is to listen carefully to our thoughts. They are not however the same thing and identifying the voice of God within our muddled thinking takes prayerful practice. All such thoughts must be tested against the Biblical revelation, wise Christian counsel, and our own previous experience of how He has guided us in the past.

There are other ways in which we can listen. Amongst them are:
- prayerfully using the Bible by, for example, questioning the text about how it applies to our lives.
- listening to the wise counsel of trusted fellow Christians
- prayerfully reading Christian books.

We grow as we learn to listen to and for "the word from the Lord".

Verse 9c
asking God to fill you with the knowledge of his will through all spiritual wisdom and understanding.

The way we come to know God's will is here given as through spiritual wisdom. Spiritual wisdom in the Bible is intensely practical – as exemplified for example by the book of Proverbs. It is all about knowing how to behave in a particular situation so as to produce the greatest good both for oneself, and for all the others with whom we are in contact. Wisdom is built up over the years by listening to God and acting on His guidance.

Understanding in our culture is related to being able to explain. However, biblically it goes beyond this to include the ability to apply wisdom to specific situations. I am reminded of my early struggles to understand Physics. We not only needed to know the Laws of Physics, but also to show that we understood them, by applying them to what seemed to be interminable (and often unlikely) examples. There is little point in knowing the Laws of Physics if you cannot apply them. Likewise there is little point in having wisdom if you do not use it in everyday life.

So when Paul prays that his friends may have *wisdom* and *understanding,* he is praying that they may know and understand the great truths of Christianity, by applying them to the tasks and decisions of everyday living. The Christian must know what Christianity means, not in a vacuum, but in the business of living from day to day. Growing in the faith is also about becoming more able to apply the truths which we know.

It is important to realise that this is as much for the benefit of others as for ourselves. The world today is crying out for wisdom for everyday living. There are magazines devoted entirely on how to live – and every newspaper has its agony aunt. Within the last few years I have personally come across many situations where a little wisdom would have saved much hurt. Ones which stick in my mind are:
- The student at summer school who slipped off by himself in the evening, found a prostitute and ended up being badly mugged.

- The girl who slept around a bit, then found she might not be able to have children because of a sexually transmitted disease.
- The young man who thought he was gay and whose much older partner left him, leading him to attempt suicide.
- The messy divorce where the partners think of more and more ways to hurt their previous spouse.

Let us recognize that we have something of immense value in God given wisdom for daily living, something for us to share with those around us. Growth in wisdom and understanding should lead to better, more fulfilling lives all around.

Verse 10

[10]And we pray this in order that you may live a life worthy of the Lord and may please him in every way: bearing fruit in every good work, growing in the knowledge of God,

How impoverished can our prayer life be! As well as issues about how often we pray, or for how long we need to pray, there is also the question of the depth and richness of our prayer. Often, we pray either very generally, or specifically only under distressing circumstances, such as illness, accident or bereavement. This verse suggests that our main concern should be that we live a worthy life which pleases God, and within which knowledge of Him grows. This should therefore be reflected in our prayers.

It also suggests that such a life will *"Bear fruit in every good work"*. Again Paul is thinking metaphorically (see Gal 5:22). Just as fruit trees grow and bear pleasant, nutritious fruit, so too should our lives bear fruit. The fruit of our life in Christ includes love, joy, peace, patience, kindness, faithfulness, gentleness, and self-control. As we grow, every good work (taking out the flowers after church, a quiet word as we stop to talk to an acquaintance, sitting with someone distressed or ill) should demonstrate one or more of these fruits.

God is also pleased, as we get to know more about Him and experience more of Him in our daily lives. This is Godly living. This is *"growing in the knowledge of God"*. Growth brings a greater knowledge of God as well as more and more of the fruits of the Spirit.

Verse 11a

[11]being strengthened with all power according to his glorious might

It is one thing in life to know what to do, but quite another to do it. For the most part, we are well aware of what we ought to do; our problem in many situations is in actioning that knowledge. We find ourselves caught in a situation where we know what is expected of us, but are unable (or unwilling) to do it. We lack either the physical power or the will power or both.

But our loving God not only tells us His will; He also enables us to perform it. If He <u>only</u> told us what His will was, we would get more and more angry with ourselves and with Him as we continually failed Him. The good news is that through prayer we can attain both knowledge and power. He can rebuild us from the inside. Our role is to allow Him to do so, as we move through the situations of our lives. The power of God at work in human lives is awesome.

Therefore, Paul prays that his friends may be strengthened with this power from God. As we pray in this vein, for both our friends and ourselves, so too do we grow.

Verses 11b and 12a
so that you may have great endurance and patience, and joyfully ^{12} giving thanks to the Father

Interestingly the reason why we need to be strengthened is given here as enabling us to develop patience and endurance. How well He knows us! How easily we give up! Our natural inclination is to expect instant results, for a number of reasons:
- Because we pray only for good things (we think!) and God is a loving God, we expect Him to respond immediately.
- Because the creator God can do anything.
- Jesus seemed to produce instant miracles in response to needy situations. Why not us? After all we are corporately the body of Christ.

Our impatience is understandable, but should not dominate our thinking. When God made time he made plenty of it! Furthermore he has chosen to limit the use of His power in order that all human beings could have free will – and Jesus did not heal everyone who was sick. If a particular project is of God, then it will be completed in His time.

One visible outcome of growth is that we give joyful thanks for the power, patience and endurance, which He provides – but there is more to it still. Paul now goes on to remind us of the many other things that Jesus has done for us.

Verses 12-14
who has qualified you to share in the inheritance of the saints in the kingdom of light. ^{13} For he has rescued us from the dominion of darkness and brought

us into the kingdom of the Son he loves, [14] in whom we have redemption, the forgiveness of sins.

Throughout our Christian life we need to remind ourselves of the basis of our faith. Paul briefly reminds his readers of this in this passage. We are qualified to enter into God's Kingdom, because of our acceptance of His actions in rescuing us. This Kingdom is one of complete goodness (light), and thus we have been rescued from the power (dominion) of darkness (evil). Furthermore it is through Jesus that we have been brought for a price (redemption) and received the forgiveness of sins, thereby allowing us to be acceptable in God's holy sight.

Without reminders of this it is so easy to slip back into old ways of thinking – to try to earn our salvation, to put ourselves first. Growth requires this reminding as a backdrop to our thinking and actions.

So let us sum up what this passage teaches about growth. The following points spring to mind:

- The centrality of persistent, listening prayer
- The need to grow in wisdom and understanding
- Fruits of the spirit become more evident in our lives
- The realisation that God provides the power to rebuild us from the inside
- The need for patience and endurance.
- Growth requires us to remind ourselves regularly of the basis of our faith

Keeping passages like this in front of us helps us to grow, and growth enriches our whole life.

Personal reflection

Give thanks for these verses, especially for any particular points which struck you on reading them.

Do you talk to God more than you listen, or do you listen to God more than you talk?

What can you do to help develop a more persistent, listening prayer life?

Are you wise? Have you recently had opportunities to offer wisdom for living to anyone? With what result?

What kinds of thing have helped you grow in your Christian life?

Work through the group questions below as far as you are able.

Group work

1. Raise any matters arising from the passage with which you strongly agree or disagree (or simply could make no sense of!).
2. What have you found i) encouraging, ii) discouraging about this passage?
3. What can we do to acquire Christian wisdom and understanding?
4. Where in your church is wisdom to be found?
5. How would you recognize an appropriate opportunity to offer wisdom for living to a friend, neighbour or colleague? Would you feel able to do it? What (if anything) inhibits you?
6. What kind of experiences would you wish your church to provide so that you might grow in love, wisdom and understanding?
7. List some of the things that have helped you grow in your Christian life. Put them in rank order. Compare your list those around you. Are there any patterns or conclusions?
8. The importance of prayer in the passage has been emphasised. Consider together the following definitions of prayer. Which are you most comfortable with? Why?

    i. *Prayer is the elevation of the heart towards God in order to avoid evil and obtain good.*

    ii. *Prayer is seeking to know God's presence in all my feelings and thoughts so that He can calm, illumine and guide me.*

    iii. *Prayer is linking those I know and love - or who I know have special needs - to God's love and power.*

    iv. *Faith is simply prayer. (Martin Luther)*

    v. *Prayer is the communication spoken and unspoken, that takes place between ourselves and God*

9. Does your regular Sunday worship help you grow as a person? Is aiding Christian growth the purpose of worship?
10. Look at 1 Peter 2:1-3. Explore the analogy of newborn babies and pure spiritual milk. What is the pure spiritual milk to which Peter refers? Have you outgrown it yet?

Quietly pray together – *silently or aloud – as you feel moved. Rest quietly in Him, aware of His presence. He will guide your prayers. He will prompt you when the time comes to close the session. It may be helpful if one person simply starts with the words "Let us pray," and closes the session after a suitable interval by announcing the grace. Before you start, think together about what you are going to pray about.*

Session Three

The Growing Church

Introduction

In the last chapter we thought about our own spiritual growth in relation to biblical wisdom and understanding. In this chapter we will consider the context within which spiritual growth most often takes place - i.e. the church - and what is necessary for a church to grow. But first a word about what the church is.

The church is *the people of God*. As such they are physically present in our lives, and in the kindness and understanding of individual church members we see something of God. This is not to say that they are any more perfect than us, but rather that they sometimes show the love of Christ more clearly in their lives than we do. At other times we may well show the love of Christ more effectively than they do. There is even more to it than this however. Paul says in 1 Corinthians 12:27;

"Now you are the body of Christ, and each one of you is a part of it."

This implies that the church is more than a collection of individuals looking after each other whilst sharing the same values, beliefs, sorrows and joys. It has a *corporate* existence. Its members are connected to each other so strongly that they are effectively part of one another, and form the body of Christ on earth. But what does this mean? What is the reality behind these words?

It surely means that the church is a real sign of the real Christ present in this world. The church has a *physical* reality. Thus, its existence cannot be denied in the same way that the *spiritual* reality of Christ and of God may be. Furthermore corporately, acting together, it shows his love, and care, and yes, at times, his sorrow too - to the community around it, as well as to its own members. But more than this, when the church prays it is as if Christ himself is praying, and corporately it should therefore be able to do all that he did. Intercessory prayer is an essential, vital part of the work of the church.

However because it is a body it also grows and we need to ask two important questions:
- How grown up is our church? and
- How can our church grow to become more of what it is intended to be?

As a focus for our thinking, we use the very early church as a model, as described in Acts 2:42-47.

The Fellowship of the Believers

[42]They devoted themselves to the apostles' teaching and to the fellowship, to the breaking of bread and to prayer. [43] Everyone was filled with awe, and many wonders and miraculous signs were done by the apostles. [44]All the believers were together and had everything in common. [45]Selling their possessions and goods, they gave to anyone as he had need. [46]Every day they continued to meet together in the temple courts. They broke bread in their homes and ate together with glad and sincere hearts, [47] praising God and enjoying the favour of all the people. And the Lord added to their number daily those who were being saved.

Verse 42

[42]They devoted themselves to the apostles' teaching...

The first thing that comes into Luke's mind as he describes the early church isn't the liveliness (or otherwise) of the worship, or its generosity, or signs and wonders occurring within it - though they are there. Rather it is how they kept listening to the teaching of the apostles. And this wasn't done reluctantly, they *devoted themselves to it*. A growing church is a learning church. We can still hear the voices of the apostles speaking to us in the New Testament. Does our church devote time to studying their teaching?

I have spent all my life in education, most recently lecturing at Manchester Metropolitan University. I am therefore very aware that University study is very much an intellectual exercise, an occupation of the mind only, for most of the time. Bible reading and study is not. Although we are expected to use our minds, no one need ever feel excluded or inferior, for primarily the Bible works on our feelings, our emotions, our imagination, and our spirits. What we learn from it is not first and foremost to do with intellectual propositions and weighing evidence in order to reach conclusions. Rather we learn more of who we are, who God is, who we are meant to be, who Jesus was and what he did; we learn wisdom and we grow through the whole experience.

Individuals grow by devotional reading of the Bible - If you read the Bible regularly, then watch out, for it will change you deep down inside and you will grow. Similarly a church whose members are devoted to reading the Bible together, will also grow.

[42]They devoted themselves to the apostles' teaching, and to the fellowship

They devoted themselves to the fellowship. They knew each other well and they cared for each other. If someone was ill or distressed in any way, then they were likely to be overwhelmed by offers of help willingly and lovingly given. I am from a relatively small rural church – maybe 60 members with an average congregation of no more than 30, nearly all of whom are over 60 years old. They are not bouncy, loud and demonstrative in their worship. For the most part, theological problems simply do not occur to them - but they most certainly know to whom they belong. And in terms of love and care for each other they take second place to none. I am immensely proud to belong to that fellowship.

We must all ask ourselves - What is the quality of the fellowship in my church? Do people care for each other? Do they share each other's joys and burdens? Do they meet together and *"devote themselves to the apostles' teaching"?* Perhaps more importantly we must ask ourselves whether we are making the contribution to it that we should. A fellowship grows by its members asking themselves (and God) questions such as these – and then acting upon the answers received.

Verse 46

If we now jump forwards to Verse 46, we find another way of building a fellowship, they:

"ate together with glad and sincere hearts"

There is something about sharing a meal together. The food somehow makes it easier to talk to each other. Perhaps this is because a meal represents a pause in the day, when other things are set aside and we can concentrate on being together and simply talking.

My wife Irene always insisted that our family sat down together at least once a day for a meal. If one of our lads was out somewhere then we waited for him – no matter how hungry the rest of us were. There were many times when this was extremely inconvenient. But she insisted and she was absolutely right, for were it not for that daily meal we would barely have spoken to each other during the day.

In the early church shared meals were even more significant. They lived in a country where famine might always be around the next corner and food could not easily be stored. Generosity with food in those days was much more sacrificial than it is now. Not only that but also, many of the early Christians were desperately poor – and some were slaves who owned absolutely nothing. The meals which Christian slaves shared would probably be the only decent meals they had.

Shared meals together are immensely important. The tradition of Church Lunches and Faith Teas has never died out – and may it never do so! If non-Christians are invited, it also becomes an opportunity to "show them Christ" in an easy, natural and unforced way. The success of Alpha courses is in no small measure due to their format – around a meal. Meals are not only a means of growth for Christians, but of numerical growth for the local church too.

We now return to the verses we missed:

Verse 42
⁴²They devoted themselves to the apostles' teaching, and to the fellowship, <u>to the breaking of bread</u>

This is generally accepted as being a reference to a ceremonial celebration of the Lord's Supper (i.e. communion, sacrament, Eucharist, Mass etc.) rather than to the breaking of bread as part of a meal. At the very least, the Lord's Supper is a re-enactment of the last meal of Jesus with his disciples in the upper room shortly before his death. By participating in a re-enactment we are powerfully reminded of the basis of our faith – namely the death and resurrection of Jesus. "Do this in remembrance of me" was instituted as a ceremony so that we should not forget the foundation of our faith.

Jesus knew how easy it is for us to slip back into old ways of thinking – going back to trying to earn our salvation by our behaviour. The ceremony of the Lord's Supper is a powerful regular reminder of what we are about. As we participate more often, so we fall less often into erroneous thinking – and we therefore have more opportunity to grow. Not only that, but we are also reminded of the Christian message that we need to carry to those around us – so the Sacrament can also be a saving ordinance in that it proclaims the foundation truths of the faith.

A growing church is a place where the breaking of bread is regularly celebrated.

⁴²They devoted themselves to the apostles' teaching and to the fellowship, to the breaking of bread <u>and to prayer</u>

The early church was a <u>praying</u> church. Prayer is being with God, having a relationship with him, being united to him, communicating with him on a regular basis. We are all fallen human beings, forgiven, but still imperfect. We get closer to God, but will never in this life actually get into that perfect relationship which both he and we crave. Prayer is the nearest we can get. Our Christian growth is a growing towards that perfect relationship.

At this point, we must take care that we do not drive ourselves down into a spiritual depression, because we do not seem to be able to pray enough. We must remind ourselves as to what a relationship involves. When my (earthly) parents were alive, I was in relationship with them every moment of every day. Nothing could take that away. But this did not mean I was talking to them every moment of every day - or even that I was thinking about them every moment of every day. Looked at in this light, perhaps we are not doing so badly after all!

The same principle applies to churches, i.e. regular prayer leading to a growing relationship, but with the added reality that:

"Where two or three come together in my name, there am I with them." Mtt. 18:20

As we pray in our home groups, prayer meetings or church services, we can rely on him being with us. We can also rely upon him to pray with us, guiding our prayers as he begins to answer them. In the process he becomes more real to us, both individually and corporately. This may not always happen immediately when we first meet in this way, but we can be certain that as we offer our concerns to Him, he will do his part in building up the relationship, for a growing prayer life *is* a growing relationship with God.

A growing church is a praying church.

Verse 43
⁴³ Everyone was filled with awe, and many wonders and miraculous signs were done by the apostles.

The early church was a church in which wondrous things happened, and this would in itself have attracted people to it. However, this characteristic of the church is one its members can do little about, particularly if miracles are only thought of as events that are inexplicable by any known science. They are supernatural, God given events, which neither the apostles nor we can perform.

However, a better definition of a miracle is that it is an intervention of God in the events of the world, which can be bought about by either natural or supernatural means. Regrettably wondrous signs involving God working through natural processes tend to be dismissed either as coincidences or natural events, which would have occurred anyway without the necessity of Divine intervention. If good comes of them they may be seen as simply fortunate or lucky events. Nonetheless, there will be people in virtually every church who are able to testify to "lucky" events in their own lives, which they cannot convincingly interpret in any other way than as being from God. Let us be alive to such events, without jealously looking to earlier days, or to other churches, where signs and wonders seem more commonplace.

A further thought about miracles is this. Look at a flower. Consider its beauty. Consider the complex relationships between the atoms and molecules that make it live and grow. For living things to live, so many things have to be exactly right. Think about the whole planet and universe in the same vein - its complexity, and its frailty. Then consider yourself, your eyes to see with, nose to smell, and the fact that these sensations produce in us an appreciative response. You have a massive, massive miracle in front of you for every minute of every day. For me that is enough and I am content.

Verses 44 – 45

[44]All the believers were together and had everything in common. [45]Selling their possessions and goods, they gave to anyone as he had need.

A distinctive feature of the early church was the way in which the believers felt they had a responsibility for each other. This led to a desire to share what they had. Consequently, they practised some kind of joint ownership of possessions. The first impression we get is of a society whose members lived together and had everything in common:

"No-one claimed that any of his possessions were his own, but they shared everything they had" Acts 4:32b.

This would not be surprising, since there were other contemporary Jewish groups such as the Qumran sect who adopted this way of life. It may be that this was indeed the case in the early church - the sayings of Jesus about self-renunciation could well have suggested this way of life. Indeed there are modern religious communities that interpret this verse in this way and seek to emulate the lifestyle.

Another interpretation, however, which some people think more likely is that they held their goods and possessions available for the church, to be sold when needed:

"For from time to time those who owned land or houses sold them ... and it (the money) was distributed to anyone as he had need." Acts 4:34b or

A later practice seems to be of giving according to one's means:

"The disciples each according to his ability, decided to provide help for the brothers living in Judea." Acts 11.29

The truth of the matter is that they did different things at different times and in different places but it would always be characterised by sacrificial generosity. This is not surprising for as they came to know Jesus better in their own lives, they would have grown in love for each other, accepted responsibility for each other and willingly shared what they had. The way their generosity was expressed would have varied with time and place but it would always have been sacrificial.

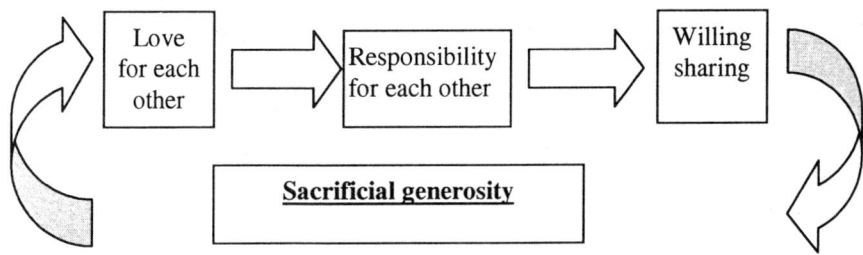

Figure 4 - Growing generosity

Generosity is both a characteristic of and an engine for growth.

A giving Church is a growing Church.

Finally let us have a brief look at verse 47

⁴⁷ ...*praising God and enjoying the favour of all the people. And the Lord added to their number daily those who were being saved.*

The church enjoyed the favour of all the people. Again this is not surprising for it had a reputation for good works and its members therefore lived in a loving, caring and attractive way. In terms of our case study of the Philippian jailer in chapter 2, it provided a strong pull factor. As a result it grew numerically as well as in both corporate and individual love for God. It was a growing church.

So to sum up the outcomes of our thoughts about this passage. The early church was:
- A learning church
- A praying church
- A church were things happened
- A sacrificially generous church, and consequently
- A growing church.

Personal reflection

Give thanks for these verses especially for any particular points which struck you on reading it.

Give thanks for your own local church, and for your place in it.

Would you wish to add or remove anything from the bullet point summary?

Consider your own church in the light of the bullet point summary.

What is needed under each point to enhance the growth of your church?

What points would you regard as priorities for your church?

How can you help bring further growth to your church?

Work through the group questions below as far as you are able.

Group Work

1. Raise any matters arising from this chapter with which you strongly agree or disagree (or simply could make no sense of!).
2. What have you found i) encouraging, ii) discouraging about the chapter?
3. What things do we most need to talk over and to think over as a church? How can we help to ensure that any necessary discussion takes place in a positive way?
4. What can we do to ensure we keep on learning? How can our church help? How can we help our church in this regard?
5. Given that there can never be too much prayer, what do you see as the problems of increasing the amount of time given to prayer a) in your own life and b) in the life of your church?
6. How can the problems identified in question 5, above, be overcome? What can you do to help?
7. Is your church one in which things happen? If so give examples. If not, has God abandoned you?
8. What kinds of things commonly cause trouble and quarrels within your church and between your church members? Are they important? How can they be a) prevented and b) overcome?
9. Read Romans 12:4-5. Does your church function as one body? Can you see your place in it?

Quietly pray together *– silently or aloud - as you feel moved. Rest quietly in Him, aware of His presence. He will guide your prayers. He will prompt you when the time comes to close the session. It may be helpful if one person simply starts with the words "Let us pray", and closes the session, after a suitable interval by announcing the grace. Before you start, think together about what you are going to pray about. Here are some suggestions*

Give thanks for the strengths of your church.

Pray for its weaknesses.

Pray that you may find your part in it (or do more effectively that which you do already).

Give thanks for individual members who have inspired you.

Pray for those you know to be in need.

Hold the church and its members quietly before God.

May you and your church be mightily blessed.

Session Four

Growing the Church

For a church to grow numerically, outsiders need to see or hear of the attractive things which go on within its fellowship. For a person to come into a loving relationship with Christ, they need to hear the testimony of believers. Testimony also helps Christians themselves grow, since there is no better way of making sense of our own experience than in describing it to others.

A growing church is a witnessing church.

In this chapter, we are going to think about our own contribution to the growth of our local church. For this we will use the words of Jesus to His disciples immediately before His Ascension, as our focus.

Acts 1:6 - 8:
⁶So when they met together, they asked him, "Lord, are you at this time going to restore the kingdom to Israel?"
⁷He said to them: "It is not for you to know the times or dates the Father has set by his own authority. ⁸But you will receive power when the Holy Spirit comes on you; and you will be my witnesses in Jerusalem, and in all Judea and Samaria, and to the ends of the earth."

Verse 6
"Lord, are you at this time going to restore the kingdom to Israel?"

In an odd kind of way I find this verse encouraging. They had been with Jesus for three or more years. They had seen the miracles, heard the teaching, and if that was not all, had seen or heard about His arrest, crucifixion, and resurrection. Yet they still had it in their heads that His role was to throw out the Roman occupiers and restore the kingdom to Israel. They were still looking back to the time when Israel had powerful kings (most notably David) to protect them.

The fact that they could make fundamental mistakes, both in their behaviour and in their thinking, over and over again, reminds me I am not alone when I do the same, and that God in his love and wisdom can and will gently correct me. The way forward is to stay close to Him.

Verse 7
"It is not for you to know the times or dates the Father has set by his own authority.

Jesus does not however correct them directly – for in a sense the kingdom of God is to be restored but back to something like it was before humankind became rebellious and went their own way. Instead He takes the opportunity to remind them of the sovereignty of God the Father and the need to patiently await His timescale.

This verse encourages me too, for I also find waiting difficult. All Christians want to see the kingdom of God restored on earth - and this will happen, but in God's own time. Our role meanwhile is to be faithful and to get on with living the Christian life.

Leave timescales to him!

Verse 8a
⁸But you will receive power when the Holy Spirit comes on you;

I wonder how many Christians get hung up about this verse and ones like it? It is easy to think you should have more power than you seem to have, and start to wonder why you haven't got more. This can then rapidly lead to feelings of hopelessness and inadequacy. We will confine ourselves to four remarks here:

- You have more power already than you think you have! The power of a Christian lifestyle for example – look what that did to the Philippian jailer. Look how that pulled him towards belief in God.
- We receive power, as we need it for God's purpose at that particular time. We must trust God to give us what we need when we need it.
- The power of our prayers changes things – though it may not be appropriate for us to know the specifics of what our prayers have done, lest we become proud and attribute the changes to ourselves.
- We may not (yet) be able to handle more power than we now have. The temptation to use power inappropriately or to become proud because we have power is very strong. Are we not being protected from ourselves?

Verse 8b
you will be my witnesses in Jerusalem, and in all Judea and Samaria, and to the ends of the earth.

From the point of view of the church growing numerically, this is the crunch statement and consequently it requires considerable thought and prayer. Beginning on a positive note, it is interesting to note that this prophecy has now been fully fulfilled since there are witnesses to Christ in every nation and on every continent. The task of making everyone a disciple has however yet to be completed, and part of our Christian life is to help complete it.

For some people this is a challenge, which spurs them on, but for others, like myself, it can be very guilt inducing. I start to wonder if I am witnessing enough. I then feel inadequate and guilty. Because I feel that way it becomes harder for me to do even that little bit that I already do. So the feelings of guilt and inadequacy grow. In effect a vicious circle becomes established.

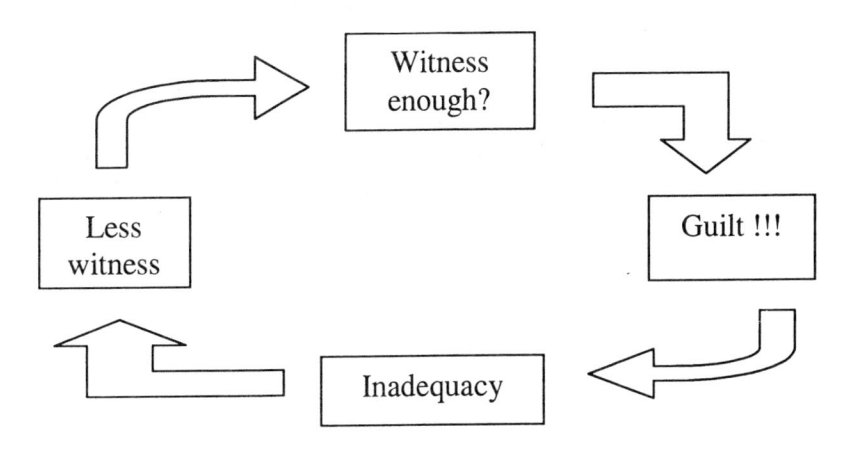

Figure 5 - The vicious circle of witness

The way out of this dilemma is to remember what a witness is, particularly how a witness differs from a preacher or evangelist.

A **witness** is simply someone who tells others what he has seen and experienced. The great characteristic is that such a person must speak at first hand. If you are ever called as a witness at a court of law, you will find that you are only allowed to speak of what you have actually seen and heard yourself. Everything else is hearsay and not admissible. Witnesses simply tell others of what they themselves have experienced.

A preacher, on the other hand, is an interpreter, someone who interprets the Bible for people today and who interprets today's experience in the light of the Bible. Similarly, an evangelist is someone who announces the good news i.e. makes known the facts of the gospel. Thus a witness is not the same as a preacher or an evangelist, though both of these may well choose to utilise their own experience within their ministries.

This is helpful in that we are reminded that the task is not as big and frightening as it first appears, after all special training or gifting, is not needed to tell someone about:

- the excitement of a football match,
- the joy of walking in the countryside,
- the happiness a new child or grandchild brings, or
- the sorrow of bereavement.

In the same way, if we have felt particularly uplifted by a church service, a hymn, or a phrase spoken in love, then all we are required to do is to say so and say how it has affected us.

A particularly effective way of witnessing is to simply invite someone to church – perhaps initially to a special family or festival service. In doing this, a statement is being made that something good is to be found there, and if they accept then they are introduced to God's people. In time they may begin to feel that they belong. In fact, there is a lot of evidence that belonging often proceeds believing in our culture. As people mix with Christians and develop a sense of belonging so they come to believe more and more, until they are eventually able to make a commitment. Believing and belonging mutually reinforce each other.

Belonging

Believing

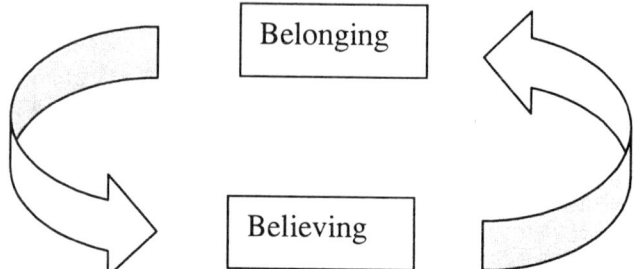

Figure 6 - Mutual reinforcement of believing and belonging.

It is important also to realise that witnessing need not be verbal. Wasn't it St Francis who declared "Preach the gospel, if necessary use words"? Thus, we witness every time we listen to someone's troubles, and every time we go out of our way to help them. The trouble with words is that people may not understand them – or they may not have had the experiences, which they describe. But they know when they are loved! The pull that the Philippian jailer experienced was much more to do with the lifestyle that Paul and Silas exhibited than with anything they said.

It is therefore good from time to time to re-examine our way of life, to see how far we really do "walk the walk" and consequently to identify with God areas for improvement. However, we must remember also that none of us has yet attained perfection, and we are not the best people to judge ourselves. The overall picture we give may be very much better than we imagine it to be!

There is one final form of witness. We need to be able to point beyond our own experience towards Christ and the gospel, if called upon to do so. This may involve a very simple form of teaching based on our own experience, and can be summarised as:

1. **Make a fresh start** (repentance)
2. **Help is available** (from a reality beyond yourself)
3. **This help can be accessed through prayer**
4. **The experience can be explained and interpreted in terms of biblical events.**

Effectively we are using ourselves as case studies. It is well worth reviewing our experience to fit it into something like the format above – we never know when we may need to talk someone through it!

There still however remains a problem that is likely to knock our confidence – namely that of why our individual or corporate witness seems in general so ineffective. However considering a diagram like the one on the next page helps.

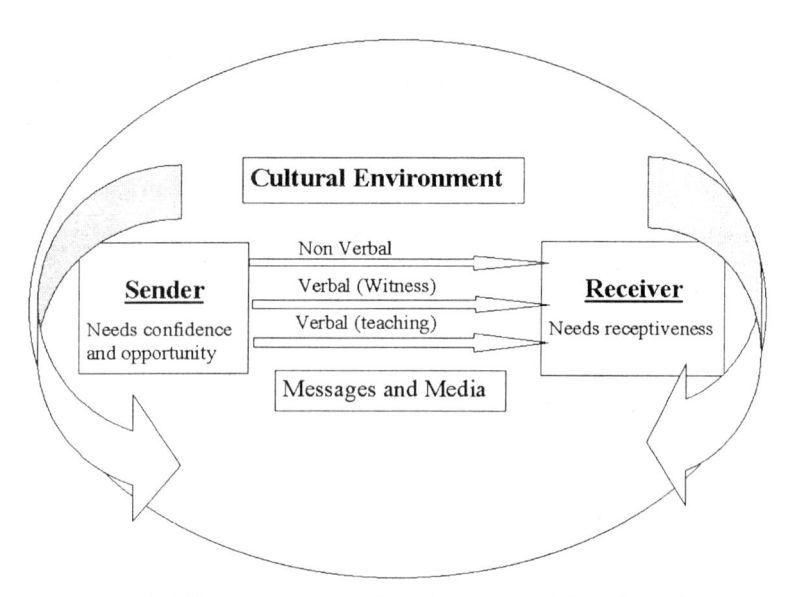

```
                    Cultural Environment

                         Non Verbal
        Sender         Verbal (Witness)           Receiver
    Needs confidence   Verbal (teaching)       Needs receptiveness
    and opportunity
                       Messages and Media
```

Figure 7 - The process of and influences on Christian witness.

This diagram shows a sender and a receiver. The sender is the Christian disciple and the receiver is the non-Christian recipient of the message. I've shown the three kinds of witness described above, joining one to the other. These are

- Non-verbal – showing the love of Christ to those around.
- Verbal Witness – telling others of our experiences.
- Verbal teaching – giving a simple interpretation of our experience.

The sender, of course, needs appropriate opportunities. Part of the problem here is of discerning the chances that are already there around us, and of having the confidence to use them appropriately. There is scope here for much prayer both before and after an encounter.

Churches are in the business of creating opportunities for individual witness. From the simple coffee morning to the church based badminton club, every activity presents opportunities. Maybe they are being missed, or maybe our church needs to start new initiatives in order to increase such opportunities. The following are some possibilities – but there are plenty more to choose from.

- Pastoral evangelism – taking out the flowers, visiting the sick, sending out greetings cards etc.

- Special course evangelism – Alpha is the best known of these.
- Seeker or nurture groups – requires good contacts and relationships in the community.
- A week's mission to our neighbourhood – need not be done in a threatening way. Makes "religion" a natural topic for a week or two.
- Community project evangelism – find out local needs and set up a project to meet them.
- Special event evangelism – occasional one-offs perhaps with a well-known speaker.

All of these are laudable and worthwhile - but it is important to realise that they are only ways of providing opportunities for a sender to send messages to a receiver. I have a feeling that if only we could mobilise all our members to be effective witnesses where they now are, this would be at least as effective as all these methods of mission.

What then of the confidence issue? This is related to feelings of inadequacy as already discussed (see Figure 5 above), but also includes various fears - of ridicule, of being asked something we cannot answer or of making such a mess of it that we set people back. Fear is not new in this context. No less a person than St Paul experienced it. Look at what he said to the church in Ephesus.

Ephesians 6:19-20.
Pray also for me, that whenever I open my mouth, words may be given me so that I will fearlessly make known the mystery of the gospel, for which I am ambassador in chains. Pray that I may declare it fearlessly as I should.

I am encouraged that Paul prays not for eloquence or the right answers, but that he might speak fearlessly and appropriately. We would do well to pray likewise, but there is something else we can do to increase our confidence. We can practise amongst ourselves. In our fellowship groups, opportunities will arise naturally when we can talk about our faith, easily and naturally with people who understand and whom we can trust. This is the most powerful confidence builder, I know.

The diagram also shows the necessity of having a medium through which the message is sent. Although I have tended to assume that the medium is face-to-face speaking and listening, we must remember that messages can be transmitted in other ways – film, video, books, web sites, audio tapes etc. It is therefore helpful to have in mind a book (or website) to recommend, should it seem appropriate to do so in the course of a conversation.

There is also the cultural environment. This presents us with particular difficulties, such as:

- The tradition of the stiff upper lip. It's not done to speak of our worries and fears in public – and this inhibits both us, and those to whom we speak.
- Religion is seen as irrelevant to modern living, and hardly worth thinking about.
- Religion is blamed for a good deal of the evil in the world – Northern Ireland, Israel-Palestine etc.
- The ideal of self-sufficiency. Religion is for the weak and inadequate (I've a nasty feeling that that was the Philippian jailers view before there was a crisis in his life).

The adverse cultural environment is a very real problem and probably accounts for much of our apparent ineffectiveness with our receivers.

What then of the receiver? I have very little to say here, except that the receiver needs to be receptive – and that is something over which we have little or no influence. In fact, there is a good deal of evidence against quick results here. A statistic, which has caught my eye is that Billy Graham's research has shown that the *average* person who goes forward to accept Christ at one of his rallies has already had 31 significant exposures to the gospel. This sounds a bit high as the figure of eight exposures is mentioned in another context.

What is clear though is that coming to faith is for many a process rather than a sudden out of the blue event. Furthermore this process primarily occurs through relationships – a kind word here, an invitation there, a discussion somewhere else, and so on. I believe that these are all examples of the Holy Spirit working in and through people to bring a person to a point where a commitment becomes possible.

Which brings us right back to witnessing. We are called to be faithful witnesses. The rest is up to God and the people to whom we witness.

Personal reflection
Give thanks for these passages of scripture especially for any particular points which struck you in thinking about it.

How do you feel about being a witness? Review some recent opportunities and how they developed.

How can you help bring further growth to your church?

Work through the group questions below as far as you are able.

Group Questions
1. Raise any matters with which you strongly agree or disagree (or simply could make no sense of!).
2. What have you found i) encouraging, ii) discouraging about this chapter?
3. Take a few moments to individually reflect quietly and thankfully on i) how you became a Christian, and ii) what your faith means to you now. Tell each other.
4. Share your feelings about being a witness. Do you feel inhibited? Why? What can be done to help us all to become more confident witnesses?
5. How do you recognise an appropriate opportunity for witness? Describe one situation where it is clearly the right thing to do. Can you think of a situation where it might not be?
6. Why do you go to church? What do you expect to get and to give as a result? What church events would you feel a) comfortable b) uncomfortable about inviting people to attend? Why?
7. Choose one of the following areas of your life such as your work, your family, your sport, and your social life. How could you bring your Christian witness to it more prominently?
8. What things does your church need to talk and think over together?
9. It is our duty and our joy to show others Christ through our Christian lives. Is there any more you individually or as a church could do?

Quietly pray together – *silently or aloud - as you feel moved. Rest quietly in Him, aware of His presence. He will guide your prayers. He will prompt you when the time comes to close the session. It may be helpful if one person simply starts with the words "Let us pray", and closes the session after a suitable interval by announcing the grace. Before you start, think together about what you are going to pray about. Here are some suggestions*

Give thanks for the strengths of your church and pray for its weaknesses.

Pray that there might be more opportunities for witness, and that these might be recognised and used appropriately.

Pray that your own witness may be strengthened.

Hold the church and its members quietly before God.

Session Five

The Sower

In this last main session we end as we began – by examining a piece of narrative. However, this narrative differs from the story of the Philippian Jailer (who was a real person) in that, it is a parable told by Jesus to the crowds of people, who came to hear Him speak on the hillsides and lakesides of Palestine. As such, it is told to illustrate a point i.e. to make the truth concrete, rather than leaving it as a set of abstract ideas. This parable is rooted in the everyday experience of the people, based on the common sight of a farmer sowing seeds in his field. It is also all about growth – the growth of seeds being used to illustrate the conditions necessary for growth to take place in people. By following the story, it reinforces some of the points already made, and also has the potential to open our eyes to see things which before we may have missed. Moreover, it is a parable which Jesus Himself explains in some detail, and thus requires little interpretation. We therefore turn our attention first to read the story as told by Jesus.

Matthew 13:1 - 9

¹That same day Jesus went out of the house and sat by the lake. ²Such large crowds gathered around him that he got into a boat and sat in it, while all the people stood on the shore. ³Then he told them many things in parables, saying: "A farmer went out to sow his seed. ⁴As he was scattering the seed, some fell along the path, and the birds came and ate it up. ⁵Some fell on rocky places, where it did not have much soil. It sprang up quickly, because the soil was shallow. ⁶But when the sun came up, the plants were scorched, and they withered because they had no root. ⁷Other seed fell among thorns, which grew up and choked the plants. ⁸Still other seed fell on good soil, where it produced a crop - a hundred, sixty or thirty times what was sown. ⁹He who has ears, let him hear."

In Palestine, as in many other parts of the world, seed was sown by the sower scattering it all around him as he walked up and down the field. The fields were usually long narrow strips, with the ground between them forming a pathway, which was a right of way for anyone passing that way. The ground would therefore be compacted by the feet of many passers by. Seed falling there would have little chance of taking root.

The rocky places were not ground which was full of rocks and stones – a good farmer would have gradually cleared such ground over the years. Rather it was ground where the earth only had a depth of a few centimetres before the hard bedrock was met. Seed could well germinate here, for a small plant requires little soil, but the soil would not hold water and nutrient and consequently the seedling would quickly die.

The thorny ground is basically good soil, but soil which had not been properly prepared or tended. It was full of the root systems of perennial weeds, the most common of which in Palestine could well have been somewhat scraggy, thorny plants. We have many similar problem plants here in the UK. I remember more than a few battles to get rid of couch grass, nettles and thorny bramble from my little vegetable plot.

The good soil has none of these problems. It is soft, deep, and well tended. It is in ground such as this that seeds can take root, grow vigorously and yield an abundant harvest.

So what do we conclude about the growth of individuals or churches from this story? If the seed is the gospel message and the soil the individual hearer, then it clearly draws attention to the need for receptiveness in the hearer and fits in well with the model of the growth process given in Figure 7. But could it also refer to a culture or sub-culture of a nation? If this is the case then the different kinds of soil refer to differing cultural environments, and the problems they can bring in spreading the message. And what about inevitability? Soil cannot change itself or its location - thus some seed will never take root and bear fruit. Is there a hint of Calvinistic pre-destination here? Before addressing these questions let us consider the interpretation given by Jesus, several verses later.

Matthew 13:18-23
[18]*"Listen then to what the parable of the sower means:* [19]*When anyone hears the message about the kingdom and does not understand it, the evil one comes and snatches away what was sown in his heart. This is the seed sown along the path.* [20]*The one who received the seed that fell on rocky places is the man who hears the word and at once receives it with joy.* [21]*But since he has no root, he lasts only a short time. When trouble or persecution comes because of the word, he quickly falls away.* [22]*The one who received the seed that fell among the thorns is the man who hears the word, but the worries of this life and the deceitfulness of wealth choke it, making it unfruitful.* [23]*But the one who received the seed that fell on good soil is the man who hears the word and understands it. He produces a crop, yielding a hundred, sixty or thirty times what was sown."*

This clears up the first issue in the previous paragraph – the different kinds of soil are clearly identified with the different kinds of hearers – or perhaps more accurately their particular state of mind around the time of their hearing the message. Thus:

- The hard pathway refers to people with a *closed* mind. The message is dismissed rather than being thought about in any depth. It is unable to penetrate the compacted soil to take root in any way.

- The rocky ground is identified with the *shallow* mind that is swept away with enthusiasm at the beginning but which does not think things through and moves on enthusiastically to the next set of ideas that happen to come along.

- The thorny ground relates to the *over-full* mind. It is so preoccupied with daily worries and concerns, that prayer, fellowship, thinking about the faith, etc are crowded out. Thus, what little growth there is, is soon choked and the faith dies.

- The good soil therefore represents the *thoughtful* mind that not only hears the message, but also carefully considers and applies it consistently over a period of time. With such a mind, a person will grow in the faith.

What then of the inevitability of it all? Part of the considerations here must be the nature of parables themselves. They are spur of the moment illustrations usually relating to one point – though sometimes, as here, they can illustrate more than one point within a general theme. They are meant to be spoken, rather than carefully crafted beforehand. It is therefore wrong to see meaning in every detail. Suggesting that soil and therefore minds, cannot be changed is one such detail when considered alongside many other statements of Jesus elsewhere in the gospels. In fact in Luke's Gospel, He calls for a mind change as a pre-requisite of salvation.

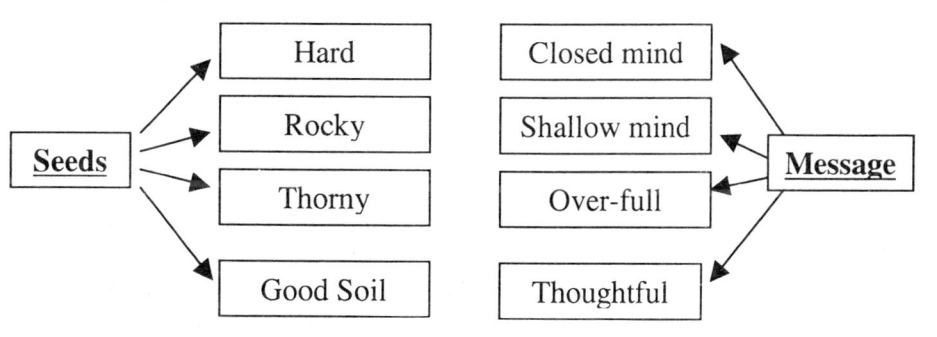

Figure 8 - The parable of the Sower

Luke 13:3
...unless you repent, you too will all perish.

Repentance means a change of mind, leading to a change in the direction of one's life. Indeed, also in Luke, Jesus clearly states that the purpose of his ministry is to bring about repentance.

Luke 5:31-32
³¹Jesus answered them, "It is not the healthy who need a doctor, but the sick. ³²I have not come to call the righteous, but sinners to repentance."

Most, if not all, of His teaching aims to create conditions in people's thinking that might bring about such a change of mind.

So then the parable is meant to provoke thought in its hearers about their state of mind and how it needs to be changed. Let us not however be too introspective. Constantly re-examining our state of mind is rather like constantly digging up a plant to see if it is growing. We can end up making ourselves feel unworthy and depressed, which does no good in the long run. Rather the very fact that we are worrying about our state of mind shows that we have already got a thoughtful mind. Otherwise why should we want to think about it at all? The parable is intended to jolt open the closed mind, not to trouble the thoughtful one!

There is however another important point, which we have not addressed up to now. The parable is given to the crowds – their need is to open their minds to the teaching that Jesus brings. They need to carefully think out its meaning themselves and apply it to their situation. On the other hand, the interpretation is given afterwards to the disciples when on their own. Jesus clearly discerns in them that they already have thoughtful minds and the parable is thus one of encouragement for them.

Matthew 13:16-17

¹⁶But blessed are your eyes because they see, and your ears because they hear. ¹⁷For I tell you the truth, many prophets and righteous men longed to see what you see but did not see it, and to hear what you hear but did not hear it.

Moreover, the encouragement goes beyond a little pat on the back for being open minded. At this stage in Jesus' ministry, the synagogues were closing to Him and many of the leaders of the orthodox religion were turning against Him. It is true that people came to hear Him and witness His healing power, but many simply went away and forgot what they had seen and heard. The disciples may well have had thoughtful minds, but their spirits could, in the same way, have been discouraged in that He was having so little apparent impact on ordinary people to balance the growing hostility of the leaders.

The message of encouragement is in the climax of the parable at the end. The open-minded hearer:

Matthew 13:23b
... produces a crop, yielding a hundred, sixty or thirty times what was sown."

The harvest, therefore, is not only secure but it will have a bumper yield. Every farmer knows that not every seed sown will germinate and grow to produce strong, healthy, and high yielding plants. Some will be blown away, some will not receive enough nourishment for one reason or another, and weeds will inhibit the growth of still others. But this does not stop him sowing nor for hoping and praying for a bumper harvest. The parable reminds discouraged disciples that in spite of the difficulties some seed will nonetheless bear fruit and when it does it will be abundant. We should always go forward in a hopeful frame of mind. Our situation may be difficult. We may seem to be having little impact but ultimately growth will take place.

There remains one final rather obvious but crucial point. The sower should not look for quick results. There is never any haste in nature's growth. Even under the most perfect conditions that modern agricultural technology can devise, the seed has still to go through the stages of germination, growth to maturity and finally the production of its own fruit. We may be able to speed it up a little by controlling the environment – but not by much!

Our task is to sow the seed and leave the rest to God.

Personal reflection

Give thanks for these passages of scripture especially for any particular points which struck you in thinking about it.

How do you feel about your own current state of mind? Which of the four categories shown in Figure 8 are you closest to?

What can you do to develop a more thoughtful mind?

How can you use this parable to encourage a) yourself and b) others?

Work through the group questions below as far as you are able.

Group Questions

1. Raise any matters with which you strongly agree or disagree (or simply could make no sense of!).
2. What have you found i) encouraging, ii) discouraging about this chapter? What is your overall feeling about it?
3. Take a few moments to individually reflect quietly and thankfully on your current states of mind. Tell each other honestly where you think you are at. Encourage one another.
4. How can we help other people to a) open a closed mind, b) deepen a shallow mind, and c) prioritise the thoughts in an overfull mind?
5. What seeds would you sow? i.e. what message would you proclaim? Would the message vary according to the person you are addressing – i.e. according to how you perceive his/her state of mind? What can be done to encourage a more thoughtful approach to matters of religion?
6. A suggestion is made in the commentary above that the parable could refer to different cultures or sub-cultures in a society. Do you agree?
7. If you agree then types of cultural environment replace types of mind. Let each person choose one of the following areas of their life such as work, family, sport, or social life. Use the categories for types of mind to describe the predominant cultural environment within that area.
8. What can be done to create a more receptive cultural environment a) in each case and b) in our nation? Is there anything we can do?

***Quietly pray together** – silently or aloud - as you feel moved. Rest quietly in him, aware of his presence. He will guide your prayers. He will prompt you when the time comes to close the session. It may be helpful if one person simply starts with the words "Let us pray," and closes the session after a suitable interval by announcing the grace. Before you start, think together about what you are going to pray about.*

Session Six
Further Bible Passages

One of the problems of following a theme, such as that of "growth", through the Bible is knowing when to stop, for there is often more to it than can be contained in a short book such as this. Much will depend, however, on the purpose in following such a theme, and hopefully this book forms at least a good readable introduction. There were two main purposes in mind whilst it was being written:

- As a good devotional read for the committed Christian
- As house group material for groups wishing to explore growth, as seen in selected passages of scripture.

I conclude by suggesting some further passages that may be of help, beginning with some case studies.

Jesus as a boy. We know precious little about the growth of Jesus Himself, but clues about His spiritual growth can be gleaned from His visit to the temple when he was 12 years old. Luke 2: 39-52.

The Temptations of Jesus. Jesus, as fully human, would have faced temptations throughout His life, but the passages in the gospels early in His ministry, show how He dealt with them. They are clearly growth points in His development and well worth close study. Matt 4:1-11, Mk 1:12,13 and Luke 4: 1-13

Thomas – Who, at some point, has not had some empathy with "doubting" Thomas? Following his life through the gospels shows a growth from doubt to faith – John 11:5-16; 14:1-7; 20:19-28. Consider especially the role of questioning and discovering.

Mary Magdalene – A similar exercise with Mary Magdalene also shows growth spiritually but this time love is the driving force – Luke 7:36-50 and John 20:11-18. The role of gratitude and experience are especially worth thinking about here.

Peter – Is there not an element of all of us in Peter? The engine of growth here seems to be the way he keeps failing – but nonetheless picks himself up, dusts himself down and starts all over again. Can you not echo with me "Been there! Done that! Got the tee shirt! Wrote the book!"? Matthew 16:13-23; Luke 22:54-62; John 21:15-19; and Acts 10:9-16.

Philip – Philip forms a shorter case study. Note particularly how his witness

leads to growth within himself – Acts 8:4-25; 26-40; 21:8-9.
These short passages are also worth a look:

Matthew 6:28-34. This is the "lilies of the field" passage. Growth is worth thinking about and studying, but not worrying about.

I Corinthians 3:5-23 is all about building (i.e. the growth of) a temple and a Christian life. What are the foundations? What are the dangers?

Old Testament passages also abound in the growth theme. Virtually any of the great heroes (David, Joseph, Jacob, Elijah.) can form useful case studies. Furthermore it has been said that the whole of the Old Testament is the story of the growth of a people in their understanding and knowledge of God. Where indeed do you stop with a theme such as this?

Therefore, dear friends . . . grow in the grace and knowledge of our Lord and Saviour Jesus Christ. To him be glory both now and forever! Amen. - 2 Peter 3:17-18.

About the Author

Colin Smith is a Methodist Local Preacher who lives in the High Peak of Derbyshire. He has been preaching for more than 20 years, and has led house groups regularly throughout that time.

After graduating from Keele University, with a BA (Hons) in Physics and Philosophy, Colin spent six years as a schoolteacher in Tororo, Uganda, during which time he married Irene. After a short spell of teaching in the UK, he entered teacher education before finally becoming a Senior Lecturer at the Manchester Metropolitan University. Following his recent retirement, Colin is hoping to spend more time preaching and teaching, and doing a little writing.

Colin and Irene have two sons, David and Andrew and a granddaughter Ashleigh.

MOORLEYS

We are growing publishers, adding several new titles to our list each year. We also undertake private publications and commissioned works.

Our range includes:-

Books of Verse:
Devotional Poetry
Recitations for Children
Humorous Monologues

Drama
Bible Plays
Sketches
Christmas, Passiontide,
  Easter and Harvest Plays
Demonstrations

Resource Books
Assembly Material
Songs and Musicals
Children's Addresses
Prayers
Worship and Preaching
Books for Speakers

Activity Books
Quizzes
Puzzles
Painting Books

Church Stationery
Notice Books
Cradle Roll Certificates
Presentation Labels

Associated Lists and Imprints
Cliff College Publishing
Nimbus Press
Headway
Social Workers Christian Fellowship

Please send a stamped addressed envelope (C5 approx 9" x 6") for the current catalogue or consult your local Christian Bookshop who will either stock or be able to obtain Moorleys titles.